CHOWDERS AND SOUPS

50 Recipes for the Home Chef

Liz Feltham

NIMBUS
PUBLISHING

For our mothers—Elizabeth McIsaac, Sue Feltham,
Una White, and Rita MacDonald.

Nimbus Publishing Limited
3660 Strawberry Hill St, Halifax, NS B3K 5A9
(902) 455-4286 nimbus.ca

Printed and bound in China
Interior photos: Scott Munn, photomunn.com (except pages iv, 3, 27, 59, 76)
Scott Munn has worked as a commercial and editorial photographer for the last ten years. His clients include Nova Scotia Tourism, Parks Canada, and CBC Television.
Author photo: Mike Feltham
Design: Kate Westphal, Graphic Detail Inc.

Library and Archives Canada Cataloguing in Publication

Feltham, Liz
Chowders and soups / Liz Feltham.
Includes index.
ISBN 978-1-55109-905-7

1. Soups. 2. Cookbooks. I. Title.
TX757.F45 2012   641.8'13   C2011-907614-4

Nimbus Publishing acknowledges the financial support for its publishing activities from the Government of Canada, the Canada Council for the Arts, and from the Province of Nova Scotia. We are pleased to work in partnership with the Province of Nova Scotia to develop and promote our creative industries for the benefit of all Nova Scotians.

contents

introduction

Chowder breathes reassurance. It steams consolation.
—Clementine Paddleford

There it is, summed up in a half dozen words—the essence of chowder. And Maritimers know chowder better than most: the region's eponymous soup can be found in virtually every restaurant, a recipe in nearly every kitchen.

This book is a collection of chowder recipes amassed over my years as both a home cook and a professional chef. It pays homage to many variations of seafood chowder, from the very traditional to the globally influenced, along with a few other stockpot favourites. Chowder can be simple and rustic or elegant and complex.

Chowders and soups are remarkably forgiving—no precise measurements or timings are required. These recipes can be followed exactly, or customized to your personal preferences. Don't be afraid to experiment and make each recipe your own.

"Soup is not like a cookie recipe, it will always turn out."
—Nina Parsons, soup-maker extraordinaire

Bon appétit,
Liz Feltham

smoked seafood chowder
Serves 4–6

This recipe calls for mackerel, mussels, and oysters, but any smoked fish or shellfish can be substituted with equally good results.

1 tablespoon olive oil
1/4 cup diced onion
1/4 cup diced carrot
1/4 cup diced sweet potato
1/4 cup diced fennel
3 cups canned crushed tomatoes
2 ounces smoked mackerel
3 ounces smoked mussels
3 ounces smoked oysters
1 cup coffee (18%) cream

Heat oil in a large, heavy-bottomed pot over medium heat. Add onion, carrot, sweet potato, and fennel, and cook until soft, stirring occasionally. Add tomatoes and bring to a boil. Reduce heat to a simmer, and add mackerel, mussels, and oysters. Stir in coffee cream.

Heat through before serving.

caribbean seafood chowder
Serves 4–6

A taste of the Islands, this chowder is very hot and very spicy, with a touch of the rum for which the Caribbean is so well known.

3 slices bacon, diced
1 tablespoon bacon fat
1/4 cup diced onion
2 cloves garlic, crushed
1/4 cup diced celery
1/2 cup diced potato
2 sweet red peppers, seeded and finely chopped
1 jalapeño pepper, seeded and minced
1/4 Scotch bonnet pepper, finely chopped
1/4 pound raw haddock fillets, cubed
1/4 pound raw hake fillets, cubed
1/2 pound raw shrimp, peeled and deveined
1/2 pound cooked, shucked mussels
1 cup fish stock (see page 79)
2 cups canned whole tomatoes, roughly chopped
1 tablespoon tomato paste
1/4 cup lime juice
2 ounces dark rum
1/4 teaspoon dried thyme
1/4 teaspoon paprika
1/4 teaspoon freshly grated nutmeg
1/4 teaspoon cinnamon
1 teaspoon salt
1/4 teaspoon black pepper
2 tablespoons chopped cilantro

Cook bacon in a large, heavy-bottomed pot over medium heat just until crisp. Drain fat, reserving 1 tablespoon, and set bacon aside. Return fat to pan. Add onion, garlic, celery, and potato, and cook until softened, stirring occasionally.

Add red peppers, jalapeño pepper, and Scotch bonnet pepper and stir 1–2 minutes.

Add haddock, hake, and shrimp, cooking just until fish is opaque. Add mussels, fish stock, canned tomatoes, tomato paste, lime juice, and dark rum and bring to a boil.

Reduce heat to a simmer and add thyme, paprika, nutmeg, cinnamon, salt, black pepper, and cilantro. Simmer 6–8 minutes before serving.

classic maritime chowder
Serves 4–6

1 tablespoon (15 mL) butter
1/4 cup diced onion
1/4 cup diced celery
1/2 cup diced potato
1 cup fish stock
2 cups milk
2 tablespoons all-purpose flour
8 ounces raw haddock fillets, cubed
4 ounces cooked, shucked clams
4 ounces cooked shrimp, diced
1 bay leaf
1 teaspoon dried thyme
1 teaspoon dried basil
1/2 teaspoon salt
1/4 black pepper

Melt butter in a large, heavy-bottomed pot over medium heat. Add onion,
celery, and potato and simmer until softened. Add fish stock and milk and
bring back up to a simmer. Whisk in flour and cook until chowder begins to
thicken. Add haddock, clams, and shrimp and cook just until fish is opaque.
Add bay leaf, thyme, basil, salt, and pepper and cook 3–4 minutes longer.
Remove bay leaf before serving.

bluenose chowder
Serves 4–6

2 tablespoons butter
1/4 cup diced yellow onion
1 cup water
2 cups milk
1/2 cup diced potato
1/3 pound raw haddock fillets, cubed
1/3 pound raw scallops
1/3 pound cooked lobster meat
1/3 pound cooked, shucked mussels
2 tablespoons all-purpose flour
1 teaspoon salt
1 teaspoon pepper

Melt butter in a large, heavy-bottomed pot over medium heat. Add onion and simmer until softened. Add water and milk and bring back up to a simmer. Add potato and cook until tender. Add haddock and scallops and simmer just until fish is opaque. Add lobster and mussels, and whisk in flour. Cook until chowder begins to thicken. Season with salt and pepper.

classic shellfish chowder
Serves 4–6

1 tablespoon butter
1 onion, chopped
2 stalks celery, chopped
1 large yellow potato, diced
1 cup fish stock
1/2 cup raw shrimp, peeled and deveined
1/2 cup raw scallops
2 cups coffee (18%) cream
1/2 cup cooked lobster
1 tablespoon chopped fresh oregano
1 teaspoon salt
1/2 teaspoon pepper

Melt butter in a large, heavy-bottomed pot over medium heat. Add onion, celery, and potato, and cook, stirring occasionally, until vegetables are softened. Add fish stock and bring to a boil. Add shrimp and scallops. As soon as the shrimp turn pink (2–3 minutes), reduce heat to a simmer (both shrimp and scallops cook very quickly).

Add coffee cream, lobster, oregano, salt, and pepper. Bring back up to a simmer and serve.

periwinkle chowder
Serves 4–6

Periwinkles are sea snails with good PR, as "periwinkle" is a much more whimsical name than plain old "sea snail." They are commonly available in midsummer throughout the Maritimes. Having a somewhat sweet, clam-like taste, they fit well into any seafood chowder.

1 pound periwinkles
3 slices bacon, chopped
2 small yellow potatoes, diced
2 cloves fresh garlic, diced
1 cup fish stock
1 cup coffee (18%) cream
2 tablespoons chopped fresh tarragon
1/4 teaspoon salt
1/4 teaspoon pepper

Cook the periwinkles:
In a pot over medium heat, bring about 2 cups of water to a boil. In go the periwinkles, and out they come after 3–5 minutes. They cook quickly, and overcooking can make them very tough.

Remove the little "door" (operculum) to the shell, and hook out the meat using a small skewer or toothpick. Set aside.

For the chowder:
Cook bacon in a large, heavy-bottomed pot over medium heat until crisp. Remove bacon and set aside. Drain fat, reserving 1 teaspoon. Return 1 teaspoon of bacon fat to pot, and stir in potatoes and garlic. Cook until potatoes are tender, stirring occasionally.

Add periwinkles, fish stock, coffee cream, tarragon, salt, and pepper.
Bring to a simmer and serve.

she-crab chowder
Serves 4–6

This chowder is loosely based on "She-Crab Soup," a traditional Southern dish. It's called "she-crab" because it features the bright red roe, or coral, of the female crab. Lobster roe, considered a delicacy by many, may also be used.

2 tablespoons butter
1/4 cup diced onion
1/2 cup diced celery
1/2 cup diced carrot
1/2 cup diced yellow potato
1 cup fish stock
1/2 cup sherry
1/3 cup crab roe (you may have to ask your fishmonger for this)
1 cup heavy (35%) cream
1 cup cooked fresh crabmeat (frozen may be substituted)
1 teaspoon salt
1 teaspoon pepper
2 tablespoons chopped fresh tarragon leaves

Melt butter in a large, heavy-bottomed pot over medium heat. Add onion, celery, potato, and carrot, and cook, stirring occasionally, until softened.

Add fish stock and sherry and bring to a simmer.

In a separate bowl, whisk crab roe and heavy cream together by hand until smooth. The mixture will be a coffee-pink colour.

Pour this mixture into the chowder, then add the crabmeat. Add salt, pepper, and tarragon.

Heat through before serving, but do not boil.

lobster and asparagus chowder
Serves 4–6

A spring chowder. Make this when asparagus is in season.

1 tablespoon butter
1/2 cup diced leek (use only white parts)
1 cup diced yellow potato
2 cups fresh asparagus, cut into 1" lengths
1/2 teaspoon grated lemon zest
2 cups cooked, diced lobster meat
2 cups vegetable stock
1 cup coffee (18%) cream
1/2 teaspoon salt
1/4 teaspoon pepper
Chopped fresh chives (for garnish)

Melt butter in a large, heavy-bottomed pot over medium heat. Add leek and potato and cook, stirring occasionally, until potato is cooked through. Add asparagus and cook 2–3 minutes longer. When asparagus has begun to soften, add lemon zest, lobster meat, and vegetable stock.

Bring to a boil, reduce to a simmer, and add coffee cream, salt, and pepper. Garnish with chopped chives and serve.

oyster and spinach chowder
Serves 4–6

If you don't want to wrestle with shucking fresh oysters, you can use canned—although you'll forgo your chance of finding a pearl.

 6 slices bacon, diced
1/2 cup diced celery
1/2 cup diced red onion
1 1/2 cups fish stock
1 cup tightly packed baby spinach leaves (3–4 ounces)
1 cup coffee (18%) cream
12–14 large whole oysters, shucked and roughly chopped into quarters
1 teaspoon sea salt
1 teaspoon black pepper

In large, heavy-bottomed pot, cook the bacon until crisp. Drain fat and reserve 1–2 teaspoons.

Set bacon aside. Return bacon fat to pot and add celery and onion. Cook over medium heat, stirring occasionally, until vegetables are soft. Put bacon back in pot and add fish stock. When fish stock is heated, add spinach and coffee cream, and continue heating until cream is just beginning to bubble.

Add oysters, salt, and pepper, then remove from heat and cover. Cook oysters in the broth about 5 minutes.

clam chowder
Serves 4–6

This is the classic Maritime clam chowder—a thick, cream-based broth with plenty of potatoes and canned clams.

4 slices bacon, diced
1/2 cup diced onion
1/2 cup diced celery
2 cups diced potato
2 tablespoons flour
1 cup clam juice
2 cups heavy (35%) cream
1 pound canned clams, with their juice
1 teaspoon salt
1/2 teaspoon pepper

Cook bacon in a large, heavy-bottomed pot over medium heat until crisp. Remove bacon and drain fat, reserving 1 tablespoon. Return fat to pan and add onion, celery, and potato, cooking until softened.

Sprinkle flour over vegetables and stir, continuing to cook for 1–2 minutes. Slowly add clam juice, stirring constantly. Bring to a simmer and add bacon, heavy cream, clams, salt, and pepper. Simmer until chowder thickens, 3–4 minutes.

manhattan clam chowder
Serves 4–6

Tomato-based clam chowders are not as popular in Atlantic Canada as they are elsewhere, but they have their place, especially if you want to enjoy chowder without the dairy. If fresh clams are unavailable, use canned—but promise to try fresh clams at least once, so you can taste the difference.

24 small clams (littleneck or cherrystone)
6 slices bacon, cut into quarter-inch dice
1/4 cup diced yellow onion
1/2 cup diced carrot
1/2 cup diced celery
1 cup diced yellow potato
2 cups canned whole tomatoes, chopped, with their juice
1 cup fish stock
1/4 cup clam juice

For the clams:
Wash clams well under cold running water. Place in a large, heavy-bottomed pot and add water just until covered. Cover pot and place over high heat. Clams are cooked when the shells are open (4–5 minutes).

Remove clams from shells and set aside.

For the chowder:
Cook bacon in the clam pot until done, but not crisp. Drain fat, reserving 1 tablespoon. Return bacon and fat to pot, add onion, carrot, celery, and potato and cook until vegetables are softened. Add tomatoes, tomato juice, fish stock, and clam juice. Bring to a boil and add cooked clams. Simmer for 2–3 minutes and serve.

lobster chowder
Serves 4–6

This is a simple chowder, allowing the lobster to be the star of the bowl.

2 tablespoons butter
1 large onion, diced
1 cup water
1 tablespoon lemon juice
2 large yellow potatoes, diced
2 cups cooked lobster meat, diced
2 cups coffee (18%) cream
1 tablespoon chopped fresh parsley
1 teaspoon salt
1/2 teaspoon black pepper

Melt butter in a heavy-bottomed pot over medium heat. Add onion and cook, stirring occasionally, until soft. Add water, lemon juice, and potatoes and bring to a boil. Reduce heat to a simmer and cook until potatoes are tender, about 15 minutes.

Add lobster, coffee cream, parsley, salt, and pepper. Bring chowder back up to a simmer before serving.

mussel chowder with tomatoes and fennel
Serves 4–6

For the mussels:
1 cup water
1 cup dry white wine
2 tablespoons lemon juice
4 pounds mussels

For the chowder base:
Mussel cooking liquid (reserved from first step)
1 cup fish stock
1/2 cup diced potato
1/2 cup thinly sliced fennel
1 cup canned crushed tomatoes
1/2 teaspoon salt
1/4 teaspoon black pepper
1/2 tablespoon fennel seed
1 ounce Pernod or other licorice-flavoured liqueur

Cook the mussels:
Combine wine and lemon juice in a large, heavy-bottomed pot. Bring to a boil.
Add the mussels, put a lid on the pot, and cook just until mussel shells open,
5–7 minutes.

Remove mussels from cooking liquid (save the liquid) and place in a large
bowl. Pick the mussels from the shells, keeping a couple in the shells for
presentation, if you like. Discard shells, leaving mussels in bowl.

For the chowder:
Add fish stock to the mussel-cooking liquid and bring to a boil. Add potato
and simmer until just soft. Add fennel and simmer for 2 minutes more. Add
tomatoes, salt, pepper, fennel seed, and liqueur. Bring to a boil, return mussels
to pot, and serve.

mussel chowder
Serves 4–6

For the mussels:
1 teaspoon butter
2 tablespoons minced garlic
2 tablespoons lemon juice
1/2 cup dry white wine
1/2 cup fish stock
4 pounds mussels

For the chowder base:
1 cup fish stock
1/2 cup diced potato
1/2 cup diced carrot
1/4 cup heavy (35%) cream
1/2 teaspoon salt
1/4 teaspoon black pepper
1/2 tablespoon chopped dill

Cook the mussels:
Melt butter in a large, heavy-bottomed pot, add garlic, and cook 1–2 minutes over medium heat. Add lemon juice, wine, and 1/2 cup fish stock and bring to a boil. Add the mussels, put a lid on the pot, and cook just until mussel shells open, about 3–5 minutes.

Remove mussels from cooking liquid (save the liquid) and place in a large bowl. Pick the mussels from the shells, keeping a couple in the shells for presentation, if you like. Discard shells, leaving mussels in bowl.

For the chowder:
Bring the mussel-cooking liquid to a boil, add 1 cup of fish stock, and return to a boil. Add potato and carrot and cook until vegetables are tender. Stir in heavy cream, salt, pepper, and dill. Return mussels to chowder and bring to a boil. Serve immediately.

Used mussel shells, crushed, make excellent fertilizer.

coconut curry shrimp chowder
Serves 4–6

Spices of the Far East meet shrimp from the Canadian East in this globally influenced chowder.

1 tablespoon butter
1/3 cup diced red onion
2 cloves garlic, minced
1/2 cup yellow potatoes
1 1/2 cups coconut milk
1 pound uncooked shrimp, peeled and deveined
1/4 cup shredded unsweetened coconut, toasted
1/3 cup heavy (35%) cream
1/2 teaspoon curry paste*
1 tablespoon chopped fresh cilantro
1/2 teaspoon cumin
1/2 teaspoon salt

Melt butter in a heavy-bottomed pot over medium heat. Add onion, garlic, and potatoes, and cook, stirring occasionally, until softened. Add coconut milk and bring to a boil. Put shrimp in the pot and turn heat back to a simmer as soon as the shrimp turns pink.

Toast the shredded coconut by placing in a shallow pan in a 350°F oven until golden. This will happen very quickly, so do not leave unattended.

Add toasted coconut, heavy cream, curry paste, cilantro, cumin, and salt to the shrimp in the pot. Stir until blended and heated through.

*For ease and consistency, a commercially prepared curry paste (such as Patak's) may be used.

scallop chowder
Serves 4–6

Nova Scotia is home to the famous Digby scallop fishing fleet, and so of course no book would be complete without at least one scallop chowder recipe.

4 slices bacon, chopped
1/2 cup diced yellow potato
1/2 cup diced celery
1 pound sea scallops
1 cup fish stock
1 cup heavy (35%) cream
2 tablespoons chopped fresh chives
1/2 teaspoon salt
1/4 teaspoon pepper

Cook bacon in a large, heavy-bottomed pot over medium heat until crisp. Remove bacon and set aside. Drain fat, reserving 2 teaspoons. Return 1 teaspoon of bacon fat to pot, and stir in potato and celery. Cook until soft, stirring occasionally. Remove vegetables and set aside.

Add second teaspoon of bacon fat to pot and turn heat to high. When bacon fat begins to sizzle, add scallops. Sear 1 minute or until scallops are a golden colour, then turn scallops over and do the same to the other side.

Return vegetables to pot and add fish stock, heavy cream, chives, salt, and pepper.

Bring to a boil and serve immediately.

squid chowder
Serves 4–6

Squid rings are often battered or deep-fried, but they're just as good when prepared in other ways! The key to cooking squid is either to cook it very quickly over high heat, or to let it simmer over lower heat for a long time.

1 tablespoon butter
1/2 cup thinly sliced onion
1/2 cup thinly sliced fennel
1 pound squid rings
2 cup fis h stock
1 teaspoon lemon juice
1 cup coffee (18%) cream
1/4 teaspoon pepper
1/2 teaspoon salt
1 teaspoon chopped parsley

Melt butter in heavy-bottomed pot over medium heat. Add onion and fennel and cook, stirring occasionally, until softened.

Add squid and cook 1–2 minutes before adding fish stock and lemon juice. Let soup simmer 25–30 minutes, until squid is tender.

Stir in coffee cream, pepper, salt, and parsley. Return to a simmer, and serve.

The mysterious colossal squid has an estimated maximum length of over forty-five feet. That's a lot of calamari.

tomato squid chowder
Serves 4–6

1 tablespoon olive oil
1/4 cup diced yellow onion
2 garlic cloves, crushed
1/2 cup diced celery
1/2 cup diced carrot
1/2 cup diced yellow potato
1 pound squid rings
2 cups fish stock
1 cup canned crushed tomatoes
1 teaspoon dried oregano
1/2 teaspoon salt
1/2 teaspoon black pepper

Heat oil in a heavy-bottomed pot over medium heat. Add onion, garlic, celery, carrot, and potato, and cook, stirring occasionally, until softened.

Add squid and cook 1–2 minutes before adding fish stock, tomatoes, oregano, salt, and pepper. Bring to a boil and serve.

> "There is nothing like soup. It is by nature eccentric: no two are ever alike, unless of course you get your soup in a can."
> -Laurie Colwin, *Home Cooking* (1988)

lobster and crab chowder
Serves 4–6

An old Spanish saying goes, "Between soup and love, the first is better." That may well be the case with this luxurious chowder.

2 tablespoons butter
1/2 cup diced yellow onion
1/2 cup diced celery
1/2 cup diced yellow potato
1 cup cooked lobster meat, diced
1 cup cooked crabmeat
1 tablespoon chopped lemon zest
2 cups crushed tomatoes
2 ounces brandy or cognac
1 tablespoon chopped fresh parsley
1 teaspoon salt
1 teaspoon black pepper
1 teaspoon chopped fresh dill
1 cup heavy (35%) cream

Melt butter in a large, heavy-bottomed pot over medium heat. Add onion, celery, and potato, and cook, stirring occasionally, until softened. Add lobster and crabmeat, lemon zest, and crushed tomatoes. Stir in brandy, parsley, salt, black pepper, and dill. Finish with heavy cream. Bring to a boil immediately before serving.

spicy shrimp and sausage chowder
Serves 4–6

1 teaspoon olive oil
1/4 pound hot Italian sausage meat, crumbled
2 cloves garlic, crushed
1/2 cup diced celery
1/4 cup diced red onion
1 cup fish stock
1 cup diced yellow potato
1 pound raw shrimp, peeled and deveined
1 cup canned crushed tomatoes
1/2 teaspoon hot pepper flakes (optional)

Heat oil in heavy-bottomed pot over medium heat. Add sausage and cook, stirring frequently, until browned (4–5 minutes). Add garlic, celery, and onion and continue cooking 2–3 minutes until softened.

Add fish stock and bring to a boil. Add potato and cook until tender (8–10 minutes).

After potatoes are cooked, while water is still boiling, toss in shrimp and cook 1–2 minutes until shrimp turn pink. Reduce heat to a simmer, add tomatoes and hot pepper flakes, stir, and serve.

monkfish chowder
Serves 4–6

Monkfish is sometimes referred to as "poor man's lobster" because of the similarity in taste. It's not a pretty fish, but fortunately, it tastes much better than it looks. The tail is what you'll find at the market—firm, white flesh with no bones.

1 tablespoon butter
1 small yellow onion, chopped
1 cup fish stock
1/2 cup sliced fennel
2 medium potatoes, cubed
1 medium parsnip
12 ounces monkfish, cubed
1 cup coffee (18%) cream
1 teaspoon salt
1 teaspoon pepper
1 tablespoon chopped fresh dill (for garnish)

Melt butter in a large, heavy-bottomed pot over medium heat. Add onion and cook, stirring occasionally, until soft. Add fish stock, bring to a boil, and add fennel, potatoes, and parsnip. Cook until tender and then reduce heat to a simmer. Add monkfish and simmer for 3–5 minutes until fish is cooked. The fish will be just opaque—be careful not to overcook, as the fish will become rubbery. Add coffee cream, salt, pepper, and dill.

Heat through before serving.

salt cod and chickpea chowder
Serves 4–6

Salt cod is an important part of the heritage of most maritime communities worldwide. This recipe evokes the tastes of the Mediterranean as well as the Atlantic.

For the cod:
8 ounces salt cod, diced
1 quart cold water

For the chowder base:
1/2 teaspoon olive oil
2 teaspoons minced garlic
1/4 cup diced yellow onion
1/2 cup diced potato
1 cup canned chickpeas
1 1/2 cups canned whole tomatoes, roughly chopped, with their juice
1 cup fish stock
1/4 teaspoon ground cumin
1/4 teaspoon black pepper

Prepare the cod:
Salt cod is too salty to use as is. Before using, it should soak in cold water in the refrigerator 4–6 hours or overnight. Change the water at least once during this process.

For the chowder:
Heat oil in a large, heavy-bottomed pot over medium heat. Add garlic, onion, and potato, and cook until softened, stirring occasionally. Add chickpeas, cod, tomatoes, fish stock, cumin, and black pepper. Bring to a boil, reduce heat, and simmer 5–6 minutes before serving.

classic salt cod chowder
Serves 4–6

Salting and drying cod was a means of preserving the fish in the days before refrigeration was commonplace. Not as prevalent as it once was, salt cod is considered a delicacy by many.

For the cod:
8 ounces salt cod, diced
1 quart cold water

For the chowder base:
1 tablespoon butter
1/4 cup diced onion
1/2 cup diced celery
1/2 cup diced carrot
1 cup yellow potato, peeled and diced
1 1/2 cups fish stock
1 cup milk
1 tablespoon all-purpose flour
1/4 teaspoon pepper
1/2 teaspoon dried summer savoury

Prepare the cod:
Salt cod is too salty to eat as is. Before using, it should soak in cold water in the refrigerator 4–6 hours or overnight. Change the water at least once during this process.

For the chowder:
Melt butter in a large, heavy-bottomed pot over medium heat. Add onion, celery, carrot, and potato and cook until soft. Add fish stock and milk and bring to a simmer. Whisk in flour and cook another 2–3 minutes until chowder begins to thicken. Add cod, pepper, and savoury and allow to simmer 3–5 minutes more.

smoked mackerel chowder
Serves 4–6

Mackerel is nutritious, economical, and sustainable. What's not to like?

1 tablespoon butter
1/2 cup diced onion
3/4 cup diced celery
3/4 cup diced carrot
1/2 cup yellow potato
1 cup fish stock
1/2 cup creamed corn
1/2 cup coffee (18%) cream
12 ounces smoked mackerel, chopped
1/4 teaspoon lemon pepper
1/4 teaspoon dried summer savoury

Melt butter in a large, heavy-bottomed pot over medium heat. Add onion, celery, carrot, and potato and cook until soft. Add fish stock, creamed corn, coffee cream, and mackerel. Season with lemon pepper and savoury, and let simmer 4–5 minutes before serving.

smoked salmon chowder
Serves 4–6

This chowder is a take on the classic way to serve smoked salmon: with sour cream, capers, and red onions. But instead of using thin-sliced salmon, choose chunkier smoked salmon.

2 1/2 cups fish stock
1/2 cup diced yellow potato
1/4 cup thinly sliced red onion
2 tablespoons chopped capers*
4 teaspoons grainy mustard
12 ounces smoked salmon
1 cup low-fat sour cream
1/4 cup heavy (35%) cream
1 tablespoon chopped fresh dill

In a large, heavy-bottomed saucepan over high heat, bring fish stock to a boil. Add potato and cook until tender, about 10 minutes. When potato is done, reduce heat to medium and add onion, capers, grainy mustard, and smoked salmon. Stir in sour cream, heavy cream, and dill. Heat through prior to serving.

*Capers are the pickled bud of a Mediterranean plant. They add a briny, lemony flavour.

smoked haddock chowder
Serves 4–6

In the small town of Cullen, Scotland, smoked haddock chowder is known as Cullen Skink. This recipe is not the true Skink, as it uses sweet potato instead of mashed potato, and herbes de Provence (a dried herb mix favoured in France) as the seasoning.

1 tablespoon butter
1/2 cup diced onion
3/4 cup diced celery
3/4 cup diced carrot
3/4 cup peeled, diced sweet potato
1 1/2 cup fish stock
12 ounces smoked haddock, cubed
1/4 teaspoon herbes de Provence
1/2 cup coffee (18%) cream

Melt butter in a large, heavy-bottomed saucepan over medium heat. Add onion, celery, carrot, and sweet potato and cook until soft. Add fish stock, haddock, and herbes de Provence and simmer 3–5 minutes. Stir in coffee cream and heat through prior to serving.

blackened halibut chowder
Serves 4–6

"Blackening" refers to searing a spice crust onto food, usually fish or chicken. It's a popular technique in Cajun cooking.

For the halibut:
8 ounces halibut, cubed
blackened seasoning (see recipe on opposite page)
1 teaspoon olive oil

For the chowder base:
1 tablespoon olive oil
1 tablespoon minced garlic
1/4 cup celery
1/2 cup peeled, diced potato
1/4 cup green onion
1/4 cup green pepper
2 cups fish stock
1 cup heavy (35%) cream

Blacken the halibut:
Roll the cubes of halibut in the blackened seasoning until coated.

In a cast iron pan, heat olive oil on high heat to just under smoking. Add halibut to pan and sear on all sides. Be careful, as the oil will be very hot and may spatter.

Once the halibut is seared (blackened), remove from pan and set aside.

For the chowder:
Heat the oil in a large, heavy-bottomed saucepan over medium heat. Add garlic, celery, and potato and cook until softened. Add green onion and green pepper and cook 1–2 minutes, until green pepper is softened.

Add fish stock and heavy cream and bring to a boil. Reduce to a simmer, add the halibut, and simmer 3–4 minutes to allow flavours to blend. Serve immediately.

For the blackened seasoning:
Blackened seasoning is a combination of spices and dried herbs used
for blackening, and can be quite hot. You can blend your own or buy a
commercially prepared seasoning.

1/4 teaspoon ground cayenne pepper
1/2 teaspoon dried thyme
1/2 teaspoon dried oregano
1 teaspoon garlic powder
1 teaspoon onion powder
2 teaspoons black pepper
2 teaspoons salt
1 tablespoon paprika

Combine seasonings, mixing well, and store in a cool, dry place.

salmon chowder
Serves 4–6

1 tablespoon olive oil
1/2 cup thinly sliced leek
1/2 cup thinly sliced fennel
1/2 cup diced red potato
2 cups fish stock
1 pound raw salmon fillets, cubed
1/2 cup broccoli florets
1 cup milk
2 tablespoons all-purpose flour
1 tablespoon chopped fresh dill
1 tablespoon chopped fresh parsley
1 teaspoon salt
1/2 teaspoon pepper

Heat oil in a large, heavy-bottomed pot over medium heat. Add leek, fennel, and potato, and cook, stirring occasionally, until softened. Add fish stock and bring to a simmer.

When stock is simmering, add salmon, broccoli, and milk and return to a simmer. Whisk in flour and cook 3–5 minutes, or until salmon is opaque and chowder has thickened.

Season with dill, parsley, salt, and pepper, and serve.

haddock chowder

Serves 4–6

1 tablespoon butter
1/2 cup diced onion
1/2 cup diced celery
1/2 cup unpeeled, diced new potato
1 pound raw haddock fillets, cubed
1 cup fish stock
2 cups milk
2 tablespoons all-purpose flour
1 teaspoon dried summer savoury
1/2 teaspoon salt
1/4 teaspoon pepper

Melt butter in a large, heavy-bottomed pot over medium heat. Add onion, celery, and potato, and cook, stirring occasionally, until vegetables are softened. Add haddock and cook until fish is opaque. Add fish stock and bring to a simmer. Stir in milk and flour and cook 2–3 minutes, or until chowder thickens. Season with savoury, salt, and pepper, and serve.

When buying fresh fish, sniff. You should only be able to catch the faintest whiff of the sea, a touch of brininess. Fresh fish does not smell strong.

maritime fish chowder
Serves 4–6

1 tablespoon butter
1/2 cup diced onion
1/2 cup diced celery
1/2 cup unpeeled, diced new potato
4 ounces raw haddock fillets, cubed
4 ounces raw cod fillets, cubed
4 ounces raw salmon fillets, cubed
1 cup fish stock
2 cups coffee (18%) cream
2 tablespoons all-purpose flour
1 teaspoon chopped fresh dill
1 teaspoon chopped fresh parsley
1/2 teaspoon salt
1/4 teaspoon pepper

Melt butter in a large, heavy-bottomed pot over medium heat. Add onion,
celery, and potato, and cook, stirring occasionally, until vegetables are
softened. Add haddock, cod, and salmon and cook until fish is opaque. Add
fish stock and bring to a simmer. Stir in coffee cream and flour and cook 2–3
minutes, or until chowder thickens. Season with dill, parsley, salt, and pepper,
and serve.

potato and ham chowder
Serves 4–6

This recipe came about as a result of cooking far too much ham and potatoes for a crowd, and looking for different ways to use the leftovers. It's robust, filling, and a great belly-warmer in the colder months.

2 slices bacon
1 yellow onion, diced
2 celery stalks, diced
1 medium carrot, diced
1 cup diced cooked ham
1 cup mashed potatoes
3 cups chicken or vegetable stock
1/2 cup heavy (35%) cream
1/2 teaspoon ground cloves
1/4 teaspoon black pepper

Cook bacon in a large, heavy-bottomed pot over medium heat. When bacon begins to crisp, drain off the fat, leaving about one teaspoon in the pot. Add onion, celery, and carrot. Cook over medium heat until vegetables are soft, stirring occasionally.

Add ham, mashed potatoes, and stock and stir until blended. Add heavy cream, cloves, and pepper. Bring to a simmer before serving.

wild rice and corn chowder
Serves 4–6

This is a variation on a chowder I learned while apprenticing with Chef Scott Vail at the Halliburton House Inn. He graciously allowed me to share it. It was originally made with wild boar sausage, but that has been replaced here with the more accessible bacon.

3 slices bacon
1/4 cup diced yellow onion
1/4 cup diced celery
1/4 cup diced carrot
1/4 cup diced red pepper
1/4 cup diced zucchini
1/2 cup corn niblets
2 cups chicken stock
1/2 cup cooked wild rice
1 cup coffee (18%) cream
2 sprigs dried thyme
1/2 teaspoon salt
1/4 teaspoon pepper

Cook bacon in a large, heavy-bottomed pot until just crisp. Drain fat, reserving 1 teaspoon, and set aside bacon. Return fat to pot and cook onion, celery, and carrot until softened. Return bacon to pot and add red pepper, zucchini, and corn niblets. Cook 1–2 minutes longer. Add chicken stock, wild rice, coffee cream, thyme, salt, and pepper. Bring to a simmer and cook 2–3 minutes before serving.

sweet potato chowder with bourbon
Serves 4–6

It may seem an unusual combination, but the sweetness of the potato balances well with the smokiness of the bourbon.

4 slices bacon, diced
2 large sweet potatoes, cubed
1 medium yellow potato, cubed
1 teaspoon flour
2 cups vegetable stock
1 tablespoon bourbon
1/2 cup coffee (18%) cream

Cook bacon in a large, heavy-bottomed pot over medium heat. When bacon begins to crisp, drain off the fat, reserving one teaspoon. Set bacon aside, return fat to pot, and add sweet potatoes and yellow potato. Cover and cook over low-medium heat until potatoes are tender. Sprinkle flour over potatoes and continue cooking 2–3 minutes. Slowly add vegetable stock, stirring continually until broth is thickened. Bring to a boil for 1–2 minutes, return heat to a simmer, and add bourbon and coffee cream. Heat through before serving.

chicken chorizo chowder
Serves 4–6

Chorizo, a spicy sausage originating in Spain, is typically sold cured, and this is what the recipe uses. This sausage is usually made with paprika, and will give the chowder a reddish tinge.

1 tablespoon olive oil
1/4 cup diced yellow onion
1/2 cup diced celery
1 1/2 cups chicken stock
1/2 cup diced carrot
1 cup washed and unpeeled diced potato
1/2 cup diced red pepper
1/2 cup diced green pepper
1 cup diced chorizo
1 cup diced cooked chicken breast
1 cup coffee (18%) cream
1/2 teaspoon salt
1/4 teaspoon black pepper

Heat oil in a large, heavy-bottomed pot over medium heat. Add onion and celery and cook until softened, stirring occasionally. Pour in chicken stock, bring to a simmer, and add carrot and potato. Continue simmering until potato is cooked. Add red and green peppers, chorizo, and chicken breast. Stir in coffee cream, salt, and pepper. Reduce heat and continue to cook, stirring occasionally, for 8–10 minutes to allow flavours to blend.

corn and cheddar chowder
Serves 4–6

1 tablespoon butter
1/4 cup diced onion
1/2 cup diced celery
1/2 cup diced carrot
1 cup peeled, diced potato
1 cup corn niblets
1 cup vegetable stock
1 cup creamed corn
1 cup coffee (18%) cream
1/2 cup oak-smoked cheddar
1/2 teaspoon salt
1/4 teaspoon white pepper

Melt butter in a large, heavy-bottomed pot over medium heat. Add onion, celery, carrot, and potato and cook until softened. Add corn niblets, vegetable stock, creamed corn, and coffee cream and bring to a simmer. Stir in cheddar, add salt and pepper, and serve.

roasted corn chowder
Serves 4–6

Corn roasted in the husk is fabulous when slathered in butter. But if you can resist the temptation long enough to turn it into this chowder, the payoff is worth it.

8 ears of corn (husks on)
1 tablespoon olive oil
1/4 cup chopped yellow onion
1/4 cup chopped celery
1/2 cup vegetable stock
1/4 cup diced red pepper
1/4 cup diced green pepper
1/2 cup creamed corn
1/2 cup coffee (18%) cream
1 1/2 teaspoons salt
1 teaspoon black pepper

Prepare the corn:
Strip cornhusks down until only one or two layers of husk are left on the cob. Roast corn over grill or barbecue, rotating on all sides until the husk has blackened and the kernels begin to brown (10–12 minutes). Remove from grill, let cool, and peel. Using a sharp knife, slice the kernels from the cob and set aside.

For the chowder:
Heat oil in a large, heavy-bottomed pot over medium heat. Add onion and celery and cook until softened. Add vegetable stock, red and green pepper, and roasted corn kernels and bring to a simmer. Stir in creamed corn and coffee cream. Add salt and pepper, and serve.

southwestern chicken chowder
Serves 4–6

Southwest is opposite northeast, and when we get a cold nor'easter blowing through, the warm spices and sunny flavours of this sou'wester will keep the chill at bay.

1 teaspoon olive oil
1 small red onion, diced
1 cup diced cooked chicken breast
1/4 cup diced roasted red pepper
1 tablespoon diced chipotle pepper*
1 1/2 cups creamed corn
1 1/2 cups chicken stock
3 tablespoons lime juice
1/2 cup heavy (35%) cream
4 teaspoons chopped fresh cilantro
1/2 cup shredded Monterey Jack cheese (for garnish)

Heat oil in a large, heavy-bottomed pot over medium heat. Add onion and cook until soft (2–3 minutes). Add chicken, red pepper, and chipotle pepper, and heat for another 2–3 minutes, stirring occasionally. Add creamed corn, chicken stock, and lime juice.

Bring to a simmer, and add heavy cream and cilantro. Continue simmering until heated through. Top with cheese just before serving.

*Chipotles are smoked jalapeños. In our region, they are most easily found canned in the Mexican foods section of most grocery stores.

root vegetable chowder
Serves 4–6

When vegetables are roasted, their natural sugars are extracted, which causes a kind of browning called caramelization. This in turn intensifies their flavours, erases any bitterness, and creates a more complex tasting soup.

For the vegetables:
1/2 cup cubed parsnip*
1/2 cup cubed carrot
1/2 cup cubed turnip
1/2 cup cubed red potato
1/2 cup cubed butternut squash
1 tablespoon olive oil

*It doesn't matter what size you cut these vegetables into, as long as they are cut uniformly so that they cook evenly.

For the chowder base:
1 tablespoon butter
1/4 cup diced yellow onion
1/4 cup diced celery
1 tablespoon flour
1 1/2 cups vegetable stock
3/4 cup heavy (35%) cream
3 teaspoons chopped fresh oregano
2 teaspoons chopped fresh basil
1 teaspoon chopped fresh thyme
1/2 teaspoon salt
1/2 teaspoon pepper

Roast the vegetables:
Preheat oven to 400°F. Spread vegetables in a single layer on a sheet pan and
drizzle with olive oil. Roast until vegetables begin to brown and are soft, about
45 minutes.

For the chowder:
Melt butter in a large, heavy-bottomed pot over medium heat. Stir in onion and
celery and cook until soft. Add flour and continue cooking for 2–3 minutes.
Very slowly add vegetable stock, stirring continually while you pour. The broth
will begin to thicken. Once all stock has been added, bring to a simmer and
cook another 3–4 minutes (this ensures the flour has been cooked).

   Add the roasted vegetables to the broth, and stir in heavy cream, oregano,
basil, thyme, salt, and pepper. Bring back to a simmer and heat through for
5–6 minutes, allowing the flavours to blend before serving.

mexican seafood soup
Serves 4–6

If you're not a hot spice lover, replace the chipotle pepper and hot sauce with chili powder to your taste. You'll still have the complexity of flavours, but without the heat.

1 tablespoon olive oil
1/4 cup diced onion
2 garlic cloves, minced
1/2 cup diced carrot
1/2 cup unpeeled, diced new potato
1 cup diced fresh tomato
1 chipotle pepper, chopped
2 cups fish stock
1 cup water
1/2 tablespoon lime juice
1 teaspoon cumin
1 teaspoon cinnamon
1/2 teaspoon hot sauce
1 teaspoon salt
1/2 teaspoon black pepper
1/2 pound raw haddock fillets, cubed
1/4 pound raw shrimp, peeled and deveined
1/4 cup chopped fresh cilantro

Heat oil in a large, heavy-bottomed pot over medium heat. Add onion, garlic, carrot, and potato, and cook, stirring occasionally, until vegetables are softened. Add tomato and chipotle pepper and cook 1 minute more. Add fish stock, water, lime juice, cumin, cinnamon, hot sauce, salt, and pepper and bring to a boil. Add haddock and shrimp and turn heat down to a simmer. Cook until shrimp turn pink and haddock is just opaque (2–3 minutes). Stir in cilantro and serve.

bouillabaisse
Serves 4–6

This French seafood soup hails from Marseilles; traditionally it is not made for fewer than ten people, and the wider the variety of fish used, the better. This recipe is scaled back a little, and the seafood is from the North Atlantic, not the Mediterranean.

1 tablespoon olive oil
1/2 cup thinly sliced red onion
4 garlic cloves, crushed
1/2 cup diced yellow potato
1/4 cup thinly sliced fennel
2 large tomatoes, peeled* and chopped
3 cups fish stock
1/4 teaspoon saffron threads
1 teaspoon coarse sea salt
1/4 teaspoon black pepper
1 pound raw whitefish fillets (such as monkfish, turbot, hake, halibut, haddock, cod)
1/2 pound mussels in the shell, cleaned and uncooked
1/2 cup cooked lobster or crabmeat

Heat oil in a large, heavy-bottomed pot over medium heat. Add onion, garlic, potato, and fennel, and cook, stirring occasionally, until vegetables are softened. Add tomatoes and fish stock and bring to a boil. Add saffron, salt, and pepper. Next put in whitefish, mussels, and lobster or crabmeat. Turn down to a simmer and cook, covered, until mussel shells open. Serve with crusty French bread.

*The easiest way to peel a tomato is to cut an X through the skin on the bottom, and then plunge the tomato into boiling water for a few seconds. The skin should peel off easily—if not, dunk the tomato for another few seconds.

zuppa de pesce
Serves 4–6

Traditional Italian fish soup, like its French cousin bouillabaisse, uses fish native to the Mediterranean. This recipe uses local seafood, of course, but retains an Italian style through the use of plum tomatoes and Italian spices.

2 tablespoons olive oil
2 cloves garlic, crushed
1/2 pound raw squid rings
1/2 pound raw monkfish fillets, cubed
1/2 pound raw cod or haddock fillets, cubed
1/2 cup dry white wine
2 cups fish stock
1 cup peeled, chopped plum tomato
1/2 pound raw mussels in the shell, scrubbed
1/4 teaspoon salt
1/2 teaspoon black pepper
1 teaspoon chopped fresh oregano
2 tablespoons chopped fresh flat-leaf Italian parsley
1/4 cup finely grated Parmigiano-Reggiano cheese

Heat oil in a large, heavy-bottomed pot over medium heat. Add garlic and cook for 1–2 minutes. Add squid, monkfish, and cod or haddock, cooking 2–3 minutes or just until fish turns opaque. Add white wine, fish stock, and tomato and bring to a boil. Add mussels and reduce to a simmer. Cover pot and cook just until mussels open. Add salt, pepper, oregano, and parsley and stir.

Immediately before serving, sprinkle grated cheese over each bowl.

southeast asian crab soup
Serves 4–6

This soup borrows components from Thai, Chinese, and Vietnamese cuisines and can be adjusted to be as hot or mild as you like by varying the amount of chilies.

1 teaspoon sesame oil
1 teaspoon minced fresh ginger
1 teaspoon minced fresh garlic
1 red chili, seeded and chopped
3 cups fish stock
1 tablespoon rice wine
1 tablespoon soy sauce
1/4 teaspoon turmeric
1/2 teaspoon ground white pepper
4 ounces cooked crabmeat
1/2 cup shredded snow peas
1/2 cup bean sprouts
1/4 cup sliced green onions (for garnish)
1/4 teaspoon hot pepper flakes (optional garnish)

Heat sesame oil in a large, heavy-bottomed pot over high heat. Once oil is sizzling, add ginger, garlic, and red chili, and cook for 15–20 seconds, stirring constantly. Add fish stock, rice wine, soy sauce, turmeric, and pepper and bring to a boil. Add crabmeat, snow peas, and bean sprouts, and cook for 2–3 minutes.

Immediately prior to serving, garnish with green onions and hot pepper flakes (if using).

roasted garlic and potato soup
Serves 4–6

Roasting garlic handily tames the savage beast, resulting in a mellow, almost sweet flavour. Roasted garlic can be used alone as a spread, but in this recipe it really elevates the taste of the humble potato.

2 whole heads of garlic
1 teaspoon olive oil
1 small yellow onion, finely chopped
2 medium yellow potatoes, diced
2 cups vegetable stock
1 teaspoon salt
1/2 teaspoon white pepper
Chopped fresh chives (for garnish)
1/2 cup heavy (35%) cream (optional)

Preheat oven to 400°F. Brush excess garlic skins off heads, place garlic heads on cookie sheet or pie pan, and roast in oven on middle rack for 20–25 minutes.

While garlic is roasting, heat oil in a large, heavy-bottomed pot over medium heat. Add onion and potatoes and cook gently until potatoes are tender (20–25 minutes).

Add vegetable stock and bring to a simmer.

Remove garlic from oven. Break the individual cloves away from the main stalk. To get the roasted garlic out, lay each clove on a cutting board and apply pressure with the flat of your knife. The garlic will squeeze out the end of the clove.

Add the roasted garlic to the soup and stir.

Remove from heat. Using a blender or food processor, carefully purée the soup until smooth. Return to pot, bring soup to a simmer, and season with salt, pepper, and chives.

For richness, the heavy cream may be added.

Garlic not only wards off vampires, but has also been used for centuries to treat a myriad of health issues, including high cholesterol, parasites, respiratory problems, poor digestion, and low energy.

maple parsnip soup
Serves 4–6

A delicate hand with the Dijon curbs the natural sweetness of the parsnips and maple syrup, and adds an air of complexity to an otherwise simple soup.

2 tablespoons butter
1 small yellow onion, chopped
3 cups vegetable stock
5 small parsnips, chopped
4 teaspoons Nova Scotia maple syrup
1 tablespoon Dijon-style mustard
1 cup heavy (35%) cream
1 teaspoon salt
1/2 teaspoon white pepper

Heat butter in a large, heavy-bottomed pot over medium heat. Add onion and cook until softened. Pour in vegetable stock and bring to a boil; once boiling, add parsnips and turn heat down to a simmer. Cook until parsnips are done.

Remove from heat. Using a blender or food processor, carefully purée the soup until smooth. Return to pot, bring soup to a simmer, and stir in maple syrup, Dijon mustard, and heavy cream. Season with salt and pepper.

cream of fiddlehead and asparagus soup
Serves 4–6

Fiddleheads—those delightful little curled fronds that signify spring is really here in the Maritimes. Sadly, the season is short for fresh fiddleheads, but most supermarkets carry frozen ones that will do nicely in this soup.

1 teaspoon olive oil
1/2 cup sliced leeks
1 cup fiddleheads
1 cup chopped asparagus (about 12 thin stalks)
1 tablespoon lemon juice
3 cups vegetable stock
1/2 cup heavy (35%) cream
1 teaspoon salt
1/2 teaspoon pepper

Heat oil in a large, heavy-bottomed pot over medium heat. Add leeks, fiddleheads, and asparagus and cook until vegetables are softened, about 5 minutes. Add lemon juice and vegetable stock and bring to a boil. Remove from heat. Using a hand blender or food processor, carefully purée the soup until smooth. Return to pot, bring soup to a simmer, and stir in heavy cream. Season with salt and pepper.

Fiddleheads are so named because the curled fronds resemble the head of a violin.

nina's neighbourly soup
Serves 4–6

Nina is my mother-in-law's neighbour, and the kind of neighbour everyone should be so lucky to have. Her soup is rumoured to have great restorative powers, and, as the older folks say, can take care of whatever ails you. This is a version of her hearty beef soup.

2 cups cold water
1/4 cup diced salt beef (beef that has been pickled in brine)
3/4 cup diced cooked beef
3/4 cup diced carrot
3/4 cup diced turnip
1/4 cup diced celery
1/4 cup shredded cabbage
1 cup crushed tomatoes
1/4 cup white rice

In a large, heavy-bottomed pot, bring water to a boil and add salt beef. Continue to simmer on medium for 1–2 hours, until salt beef is tender. Salt beef is, as the name says, salty, so after the beef has cooked, be sure to taste the water for saltiness. The cooking water may be replaced with fresh water if so desired—it's up to each cook's personal salt preference.

   To the water and salt beef, add the cooked beef, carrot, turnip, celery, and cabbage, and continue boiling until vegetables are cooked, about 20–25 minutes. Add crushed tomatoes and rice, and simmer for an additional 15–20 minutes, until rice is cooked.

homestyle turkey soup
Serves 4–6

Designed to use up leftovers, this tasty turkey soup is comfort food at its best.

3 cups turkey stock (prepare as per chicken stock)
1/3 cup uncooked pearl barley
1/2 cup diced carrot
1/2 cup diced onion
1/2 cup diced celery
1/4 cup green peas
1 cup diced cooked turkey
1 tablespoon chopped fresh parsley
1/4 cup turkey stuffing (optional, but if you have some left over, throw it in!)
1/4 teaspoon dried sage leaves
1 teaspoon salt
1/2 teaspoon pepper

In a large, heavy-bottomed pot over high heat, bring turkey stock to a boil. Add barley, reduce heat to low, cover, and simmer 25–30 minutes, stirring occasionally.

Then add carrot, onion, and celery and continue to simmer uncovered for another 25–30 minutes. The barley should be soft and the vegetables should be tender.

Add green peas, cooked turkey, and parsley.

If you are using stuffing, add it now, and adjust the amounts of sage, salt, and pepper depending on the flavour of the stuffing. If you are not using stuffing, then just add the sage, salt, and pepper.

Bring to a boil, reduce heat, and serve.

german sauerkraut soup
Serves 4–6

This soup features the fabulous Tancook Island sauerkraut made on Nova Scotia's South Shore.

1 tablespoon butter
1 yellow onion, chopped
2 cloves garlic, chopped
4 cups vegetable stock
1 smoked ham hock
2 tablespoons all-purpose flour
1/2 pound sauerkraut, drained and rinsed
1 cup canned white beans
1/2 cup sour cream

Heat butter in large, heavy-bottomed pot over medium heat. Cook onion and garlic until softened. Add vegetable stock and bring to a simmer. Add ham hock, cover, and let simmer for about 1 hour; this gives the ham hock time to tenderize and share its flavour.

Whisk in flour and cook 2–3 minutes, until soup starts to thicken. Add sauerkraut and white beans. Immediately prior to serving, bring to a boil and stir in sour cream.

chilled blueberry soup
Serves 4–6

If fresh local berries are unavailable, frozen will do nicely for this simple, refreshing soup.

2 cups blueberries, fresh or frozen
1/2 cup sour cream
1 teaspoon lime juice
1/4 cup orange juice
2 tablespoons Grand Marnier or other orange-flavoured liqueur
Fresh mint leaves (for garnish)

Purée blueberries using a blender or food processor. In a non-metal bowl, combine puréed blueberries, sour cream, lime juice, orange juice, and liqueur.
  Refrigerate for 1–2 hours. Garnish with mint leaves before serving.

Oxford, Nova Scotia, is known as the wild blueberry capital of Canada. Blueberries are a so-called "superfood" because they are packed with antioxidants.

"Cold soup is a very tricky thing and it is the rare hostess who can carry it off. More often than not the dinner guest is left with the impression that had he only come in a little earlier he could have gotten it while it was still hot." -Fran Lebowitz

chilled strawberry soup with black pepper
Serves 4–6

Local berries are essential for this recipe; take a pass on bland imported berries that tend to be larger in size, but much smaller in flavour

2 cups chopped strawberries
1 tablespoon Madeira (a type of fortified wine. If unavailable, use port wine)
2 tablespoons balsamic vinegar
1/2 cup plain yogourt
1 teaspoon fresh cracked black peppercorns
Sprigs of fresh lemon thyme for garnish

In a large plastic or glass bowl, toss berries with Madeira and balsamic vinegar. Let sit at room temperature for 15–20 minutes; this will allow the berries to absorb the Madeira and vinegar.

When the 15–20 minutes are up, set the bowl aside and purée the berries in a blender or food processor. Return the purée to the bowl and stir in yogourt and black pepper.

Refrigerate for 1–2 hours. Garnish with fresh thyme before serving.

stock recipes

Stocks are the foundation of all good soup. They add body, richness, and depth of flavour.

The availability and quality of prepared stocks make it tempting for time-squeezed cooks to pick up instant stock at the supermarket, but making your own stock is so simple and the results so superior, why not make it yourself? Stocks freeze well, so you can make a large batch and then freeze in smaller containers for use when making soup.

If you do choose the convenience product, make sure it is a low-sodium brand.

Ingredients for all stocks
Bones (beef, chicken, fish)
Water (always cold, makes for a clearer stock)
Mirepoix (see glossary)
Sachet (see glossary)

A word on beef bones: when buying bones for stock, any bones will do but the best bones are those higher in cartilage, such as beef tails and marrow bones. These will add more flavour and give your stock more body.

Beef Stock (makes 2 gallons)

10 pounds beef bones (marrow or stewing bones)
1 pound onion, chopped
1/2 pound carrot, chopped
1/2 pound celery, chopped
l pound tomatoes or 8 ounces tomato purée
10–12 quarts water, cold

Preheat oven to 400°F, and roast bones in a large pan for 1 hour. Add onions, carrots, and celery to pan and spread tomato purée (if using) on bones. Continue roasting for 30 minutes. After vegetables have been roasting for 30 minutes, immediately transfer bones and vegetables to a large stock pot. Add tomatoes (if using instead of purée).

Cover bones and vegetables with cold water and bring to a simmer. As fat or foam develops on the surface of the stock, skim it off; continue to simmer for 6–8 hours, skimming as necessary. Add cold water, as needed, to keep bones covered.

For a clearer stock, line a sieve, china cap, or colander with cheesecloth and pour the stock through this to filter. Cool and refrigerate.

For lamb or game stock, substitute lamb bones or game bones (deer, moose) for beef stock.

Chicken stock (makes 2 gallons)

10 pounds chicken bones
10–12 quarts water, cold
1 pound onion, chopped
1/2 pound carrot, chopped
1/2 pound celery, chopped

Place bones in large stockpot, and cover with cold water. Bring to a simmer and add onions, carrots, and celery.

Cover bones and vegetables with cold water and bring back up to a simmer. As fat or foam develops on the surface of the stock, skim it off; continue to simmer for 3–4 hours, skimming as necessary. Add cold water, as needed, to keep bones covered.

For a clearer stock, line a sieve, china cap, or colander with cheesecloth and pour the stock through this to filter.

Cool and refrigerate.

Roasting the chicken bones will give a deeper flavour and a darker coloured stock; for a lighter coloured stock, do not roast the bones, and eliminate the carrots.

Vegetable stock
(makes 2 gallons)

2 tablespoons vegetable oil
1 pound onion, chopped
1/2 pound carrot, chopped
1/2 pound celery, chopped
8 ounces leeks, chopped
4 ounces mushrooms, chopped
4 ounces turnip, chopped
2 ounces fennel, chopped

In a large stock pot over medium heat, add vegetable oil. Add carrots, celery, leeks, mushrooms, turnip, and fennel and cook until just softened. Cover vegetables with cold water and simmer.

Simmer 30–45 minutes, skimming the top of any foam or fat.

For a clearer stock, line a sieve, china cap, or colander with cheesecloth and pour the stock through this to filter.

Cool and refrigerate.

Fish stock (makes 1 gallon)

1 ounce butter
4 ounces onions, chopped fine
2 ounces celery, chopped fine
2 ounces carrot, chopped fine
4–6 pounds fish bones (use lean fish bones such as haddock)
1 gallon cold water
sachet (see glossary)

Sachet:
1/2 bay leaf
1/4 teaspoon peppercorns
6 parsley stems
1 whole clove

Melt butter in a large heavy-bottomed pot over low heat. Add onions, celery, and carrots, then place the fish bones on top of the vegetables. Cover loosely with parchment or waxed paper.

Cook about 5 minutes over low heat. The bones will begin to release liquid. At this point, add cold water and sachet.

Simmer for 30–45 minutes. Remove sachet, cool, and refrigerate stock.

4 ounces white wine may be added to the fish stock above. This would then be called fish fumet.

You can certainly make fish stock without sweating the vegetables, but it will not have as strong a flavour.

A shellfish stock can be made using 10 pounds of crustacean shells (such as lobster) in place of the fish bones.

glossary

Chowder A thick, chunky seafood soup. From the French *chaudière*, a cauldron in which fishermen prepared stews made from their daily catch. The term "chowder" has come to include *any* thick soup containing chunks of food, such as corn chowder.

Cream Cream is categorized based on its milk fat (MF) content—the higher the MF, the thicker the cream.
Heavy (whipping) cream: 35% MF
Coffee cream: 18% MF
Blend: 10% MF
Light cream: 5% MF
(Note that 18% cream is called "light cream" in the U.S. Look for the percentage to ensure you're using the right kind of cream.)

Fin fish Broadly, fish that have fins, backbones, and gills.
There are two general types of fin fish:
Round fish have one eye on each side of their heads. They are round and swim upright (e.g. cod or salmon).
Flatfish have both eyes on one side of their heads, and swim flat on their sides (e.g. halibut or flounder).

Mirepoix A mixture of diced carrots, celery, and onion that is used to provide a flavour base for stocks and sauces. The usual ratio is 2:2:1 for carrots, celery, and onion in that order.

Sachet A little bundle of spices and herbs tied up in a cheesecloth bag. A sachet is used to add flavour to stocks, and is intended to be removed at the end of cooking time.

Seafood All edible fish and shellfish that come from the sea. A seafood chowder would have both, e.g. clams and haddock.

Shellfish Broadly, seafood that has some type of shell.
There are two basic categories of shellfish:
Crustaceans (e.g. crabs or lobsters)
Molluscs, which divide into the subcategories:
bivalves (e.g. mussels)
cephalopods (e.g. squid)
gastropods (e.g. periwinkles)

Stock In the most basic terms, stock is the strained liquid that is the result of cooking vegetables, meat, or fish in water with other seasoning ingredients.

recipe index

Other Cookbooks from Nimbus Publishing

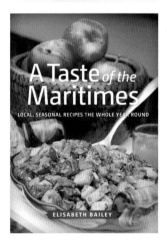

NIMBUS
PUBLISHING